Exclusive distributors:
Music Sales Corporation
225 Park Avenue South, New York, NY 10003, USA
Music Sales Limited
8/9 Frith Street, London W1V 5TZ, England
Music Sales Pty. Limited
120 Rothschild Avenue, Rosebery, NSW 2018, Australia

PAUL SIMON COMPLETE
VOLUME ONE

Cover design by Pearce Marchbank Studio, London.
Volume one of a two-volume set

US ISBN 0.8256.3310.9
UK ISBN 0.7119.1663.2
Order No. PS 11113
Slipcase Edition:
US ISBN 0.8256.3309.5
UK ISBN 0.7119.1662.4
Order No. PS 11105

All Around The World
Or The Myth Of Fingerprints

Words and Music by PAUL SIMON

5

6

Allergies

Words and Music by PAUL SIMON

America

Words and Music by PAUL SIMON

Bright waltz tempo

"Let us be lov-ers, We'll mar-ry our for-tunes to-geth-er.

I've got some real es-tate

Here in my bag." So we

bought a pack of cig - a - rettes,_____ And Mrs._____ Wag - ner's

pies,_____ And walked off_____ to look for A -

mer - i - ca._____

"Kath - y," I said, As we

American Tune

Words and Music by PAUL SIMON

al - right, it's al - right.__ You can't be for - ev - er blessed.___

Still, to - mor - row's goin'__ to be an - oth - er work — — ing day, And I'm

try - ing to get__ some rest,___ That's all I'm try - ing, to get some__

rest.

ritard.

Ace In The Hole

Words and Music by PAUL SIMON

Some peo-ple say Je-sus, that's the ace in the hole.___
Two hun-dred dol-lars, that's my ace in the hole.___ When I'm
Once I was cra-zy, and my ace in the hole was that I
Some peo-ple say mu-sic, that's their ace in the hole,___ just your

I'm___ your___ guar - an - tee.___

April Come She Will

Words and Music by PAUL SIMON

At The Zoo

Words and Music by PAUL SIMON

Armistice Day

Words and Music by PAUL SIMON

Baby Driver

Words and Music by PAUL SIMON

Moderate bright tempo

1. My dad - dy was a fam - i - ly bass - man, My ma -
2. (My) dad - dy was a prom - i - nent frog - man, My ma -
3. (My) dad - dy got a big pro - mo - tion, My ma -

ma was an en - gi - neer, ___ And I ___ was born ___ one dark ___
ma's in the Na - val re - serve, ___ When I ___ was young ___ I car -
ma got a raise in pay, ___ There's no ___ one home, ___ we're all ___

The Boy In The Bubble

Words by PAUL SIMON
Music by PAUL SIMON and FORERE MOTLOHELOA

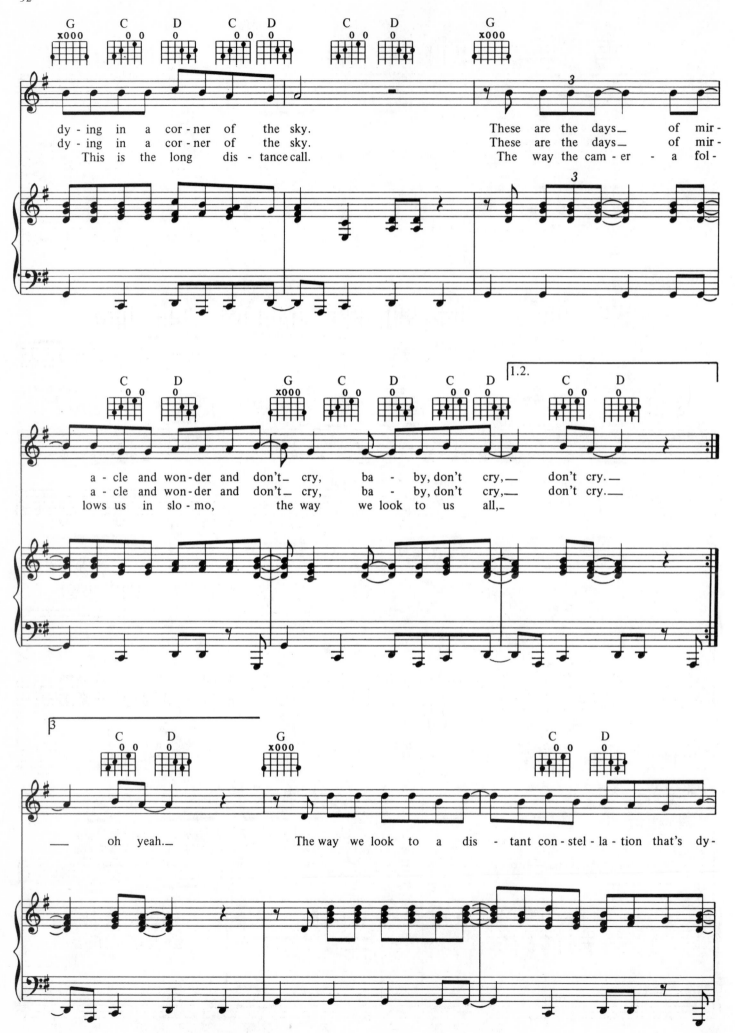

ing in a cor-ner of the sky. These are the days— of mir-

a-cle and won-der and don't— cry, ba-by, don't cry,— don't cry,— don't cry.

Repeat and fade

The Big Bright Green Pleasure Machine

Words and Music by PAUL SIMON

Well, there's no need to com- plain, ____ We'll e-
Are you wor- ried and dis- tressed? ____ Can't
We can end your dai- ly strife ____ at a

lim- i- nate your pain. ____ We can neu- tral- ize ____ your brain. ____
seem to get no rest? ____ Put our prod- uct to ____ the test. ____
rea- son- a- ble price. ____ You've seen it ad- ver- tised ____ in 'Life.'

You'll feel just ____ fine ____ now. ____

Buy a Big Bright ____ Green ____

Blessed

Words and Music by PAUL SIMON

Bookends

Words and Music by PAUL SIMON

Time it was, And what a time it was, it was A time of in-no-cence, A time of con-fi-den-ces.

The Boxer

Words and Music by PAUL SIMON

I am just a poor boy. Though my sto - ry's sel - dom told, I have squan-dered my re - sis - tance for a pock - et - ful of mum - bles, such are prom - is - es.

All lies and jest, still a man hears what he wants to hear, ___ And dis - re - gards the rest. _____

When I left my home and my fam - i - ly, ___ I was

Bridge Over Troubled Water

Words and Music by PAUL SIMON

Congratulations

Words and Music by PAUL SIMON

- mance.___

Love will do you in, and love will wash you out, and need-less to say you

won't stand a chance,___ and you won't stand a chance.___

I'm hun-gry for learn - - in',

Cars Are Cars

Words and Music by PAUL SIMON

Cars are cars all o-ver the world.___ Cars are cars___ all o-ver the world.___

Sim - i - lar - ly made.___
En - gine in the front.___
Drive 'em on the left.___

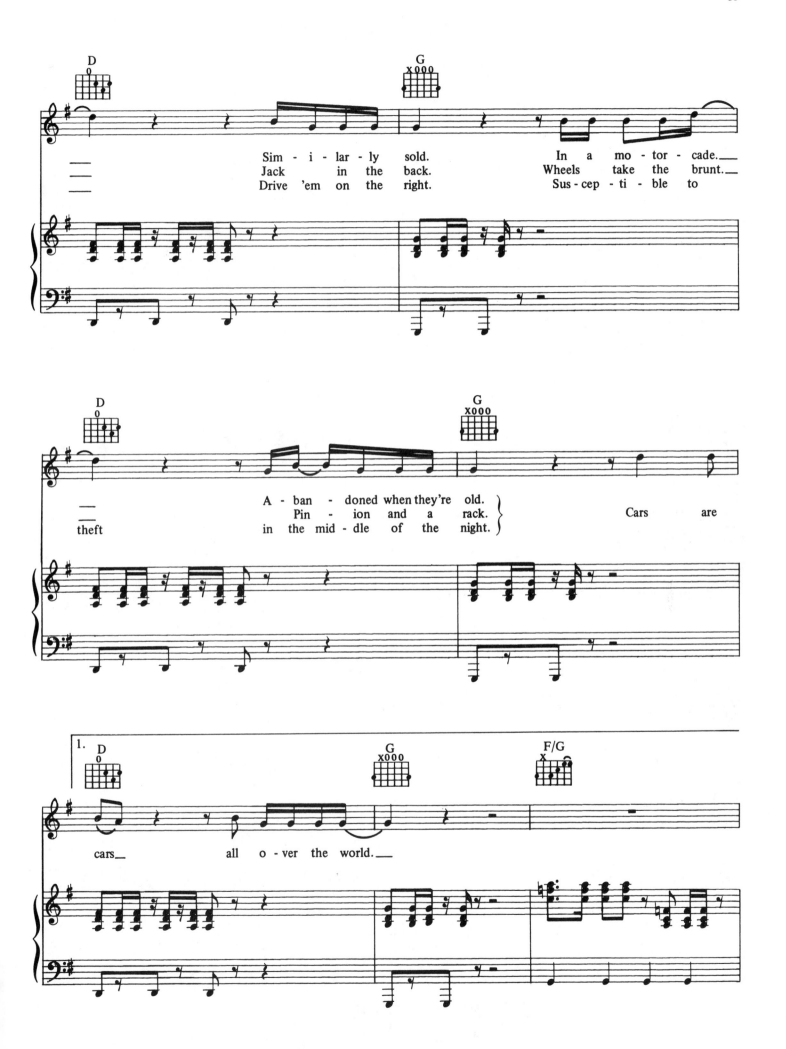

84

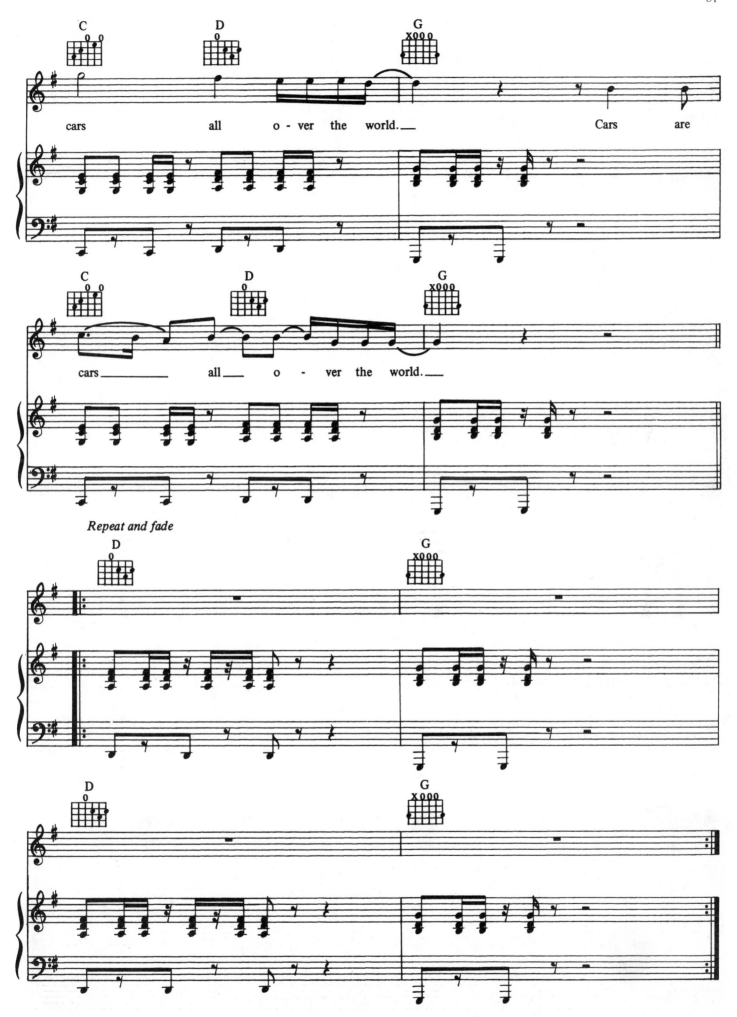

cars all o - ver the world.___ Cars are

cars_____ all ___ o - ver the world.___

Repeat and fade

Cecilia

Words and Music by PAUL SIMON

Moderate, not too fast, rhythmically

Cel - ia, you're break-ing my heart,_ You're shak-ing my con - fi-dence dai -

- ly. _ Oh, Ce - cil - ia, I'm down on my knees,_ I'm

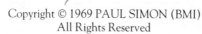

A Church Is Burning

Words and Music by PAUL SIMON

Moderately bright tempo

burn down my church-es___ but I shall be___ free." ___

Verse:

2. Three hood-ed men, their hands lit the
3. A church is more than just tim-ber and

spark Then they fad-ed in the night and they van-ished in the dark And in the
stone And free-dom is a dark road___ when you're walk-ing it a-lone; But the

cool light of morn-ing there's noth-ing that re-mains But the
fu-ture is now and it's time to take a stand So the

Cloudy

Words and Music by PAUL SIMON

Crazy Love, Vol. II

Words and Music by PAUL SIMON

The Dangling Conversation

Words and Music by PAUL SIMON

Moderately in 2

still life wa - ter col - or, _____ of a now late af - ter -
read your Em - 'ly Dick-in - son, _____ and I my Rob -ert
speak of things that mat - ter, _____ with words that must be

Melody

Diamonds On The Soles Of Her Shoes

Words and Music by PAUL SIMON
Beginning by PAUL SIMON and JOSEPH SHABALALA

Peo-ple say I'm cra-zy, I got dia-monds on the soles_ of my shoes. Well,_

that's one way to lose these walk-ing blues. Dia-monds on the soles_ of my shoes.

Repeat and fade

Ta na na na na, ta na na na na.

Duncan

Words and Music by PAUL SIMON

118

Head - ed down the turn - pike for New Eng - land,__ sweet New Eng - land.

Instrumental solo

3. Holes in my con - fi - dence,__ holes in the knees of my jeans, I's

left with-out___ a pen - ny in my pock - et, Oo hoo hoo___ wee,___ I's a - bout

des - ti -tut - ed as a kid could be,___ And I wished I wore a ring so I could

hock it,____ I'd like to hock it. 4. A

young girl in a park-ing lot___ was preach - in' to a crowd,___ sing - in'

play - in' my gui - tar,___ ly - ing un - der - neath the stars,___ Just

thank - in' the Lord for my fin - gers,___ for my fin - gers.

Fade out

El Condor Pasa
(If I Could)

English Lyric by PAUL SIMON
Musical arrangement by JORGE MILCHBERG and DANIEL ROBLES

The 59th Street Bridge Song
(Feelin' Groovy)

Words and Music by PAUL SIMON

Moderately

Eb Bb Cm7sus Bb Eb Bb

Slow down, ___ you move too fast. ___ You got to make the morn-

Cm7sus Bb Eb Bb Cm7sus Bb

-ing last. ___ Just kick-in' down the cob-ble stones, ___

Everything Put Together Falls Apart

Words and Music by PAUL SIMON

Fakin' It

Words and Music by PAUL SIMON

Pri - or to this life - time___ I sure - ly was a tail - or. Look at

me.___

(Spoken): Good morning, Mr. Leach, have you had a busy day? I own a tail - or's face and hands,

I am the tail - or's face and hands.

Fifty Ways To Leave Your Lover

Words and Music by PAUL SIMON

Flowers Never Bend With The Rainfall

Words and Music by PAUL SIMON

God Bless The Absentee

Words and Music by PAUL SIMON

Lord, I am a work - ing man and mu-sic is my trade._
Lord, I am a sur - geon and mu-sic is my knife._

For Emily, Whenever I May Find Her

Words and Music by PAUL SIMON

cheeks flushed with the night. We walked on

frost - ed fields ___ of ju - ni - per and lamp - light,

I ___ held your hand. _____

And when I a - woke and felt you warm and near,

A Hazy Shade Of Winter

Words and Music by PAUL SIMON

Moderate tempo

Time, time, time, See what's be - come of me, while I looked a - round for my pos - si - bil - i - ties, I was so

Gone At Last

Words and Music by PAUL SIMON

The night was

black, the road was i - cy, and the snow was fall - in', and the drifts were
dumb, I've kicked a - round some; I don't fall too eas - i -
while from the mid-dle of no - where, when you don't ex - pect it and you're un - pre -

high. And I was wea - ry from my driv - in'___ and I
ly. But that boy looked so de - ject - ed,___ he just
pared some - bod - y will come and lift you high - er,___ and your

Graceland

Words and Music by PAUL SIMON

The Mis - sis - sip - pi Del - ta was shin - ing like a Na - tion - al gui-

tar.

I am fol - low - ing the riv - er down the

high-way through the cra - dle of the Civ - il War.

I'm go - ing to Grace-

will be re - ceived in Grace - land.
will be re - ceived in Grace - land.
will be re - ceived in Grace - land.

To Coda

She comes back to tell me she's gone.
There is a girl in New York Cit - y who

As if I did - n't know that, as if I did - n't know my own
calls her - self the hu - man tram - po - line, and

168

Gumboots

Words by PAUL SIMON
Music by PAUL SIMON and JONHJON MKHALALI

I was hav-ing this dis-cus-sion in a tax-i head-ing

It was in the ear-ly morn-ing hours when I fell in-to a

I was walk-ing down the street when I thought I heard this

down-town,— re-ar-rang-ing my po-

phone call.— Be-liev-ing I had su-per-nat-u-ral

voice say,— "Say, ain't we walk-in' down the

si - tion on this friend of mine who'd had a lit - tle bit of a break - down.
pow - ers, I slammed in - to a brick wall.
same street to - geth - er on the ver - y same day?"

I said, "Break - downs come and break - downs go, so
I said, "Is this my prob - lem? Is this my fault?" If
I said, "Hey, Se - ño - ri - ta, that's as - tute," I said,

what are you go'n' to do a - bout it? That's what I'd like to know."
that's the way it's go'n' to be I wan - na call the whole thing to a halt.
"Why don't we get to - geth - er and call our - selves an in - sti - tute."

You don't feel you could love— me, but I feel you could.

You don't feel you could love—

— me, but I feel you could.

You don't feel you could love— me, but I feel you

could.

D.S. 𝄋 (lyric 1) and fade

Have A Good Time

Words and Music by PAUL SIMON

Moderately, with a Blues feeling

Yes - ter - day it was my birth - day; I hung one more year on the line.
noi - a strikes deep in the heart - land, but I think it's all o - ver - done.
laugh - ing my way to dis - as - ter; may - be my race has been run.

I should be de - pressed; my life's a mess, but I'm
Ex - ag - ger - at - ing this, ex - ag - ger - at - ing that; they
May - be I'm blind to the fate of man - kind, but

Hearts And Bones

Words and Music by PAUL SIMON

One and one - half wan - der - ing Jews,_____
back to__ the sea - son be - fore,_____
One and one - half wan - der - ing Jews_____

free to wan - der wher - ev - er__ they
look - ing back__ through the cracks in__ the
re - turned__ to their nat - u - ral

Hey, Schoolgirl

Words and Music by PAUL SIMON and ARTHUR GARFUNKEL

Hey, School - girl in the sec - ond row, The teach - er's look - in' o - ver so I got to whis - per way down low,

to say, "Who-bop-a-loo-chi-bop, let's meet af-ter school at

three." _____

1. She said, "Hey, babe, but there is one thing more,___
2. She said, "Hey, babe, I got-ta lot to do,___

My school is o-ver at a half-past four,___ May-be when we're old-er, then
It takes me ho-urs till my home-work's thru,___ Some-day we'll go stead-y, so

we can date,___ Ooh, _____ let's wait!"
don't you fret,___ Ooh, _____ not yet!"

Hobo's Blues

Music by PAUL SIMON and STEPHANE GRAPPELLI

Moderately, with a bounce

Instrumental Solo

Homeless

Words and Music by PAUL SIMON and JOSEPH SHABALALA

Home - less,_ home - less._ Moon - light sleep - ing on a

mid - night lake._ Home - less,_ home - less._

Moon - light sleep - ing on a mid - night lake._ We are home - less,_ we are

home - less._ The moon - light sleep - ing on a mid - night lake._ And we are

home - less,__ home-less, home - less.__ The moon - light sleep - ing on a

mid - night lake. Zi - o ya - mi zi - o ya - mi n-hli - zi - yo ya - mi n-hli-

zi - yo ya - mi a - ma - kha - za asengi bu - le - le n-hli - zi - yo ya - mi n-hli-

zi - yo ya - mi n-hli - zi - yo ya - mi angi - bu - le - le a - ma - kha - za n-hli-

loo loo— too loo loo— too loo loo loo— loo loo loo
loo loo loo.— Strong wind— de-stroy our— home.—
Man-y dead— to-night, it could be you.— Strong wind— de-
stroy our— home.— Man-y dead— to-night, it could be you.— And we are

home - less,_ home - less._ Moon - light sleep - ing on a

mid - night lake._ And we are home - less,_ home - less._

Moon - light sleep - ing on a mid - night lake._ Home - less,_

home - less._ The moon - light sleep - ing on a mid - night lake._

Some - bod - y say (ih - hih - ih - hih - ih). Some - bod - y cry

why, why,__ why?___ Ku - lu - ma - ni ku - lu

mani ku - lu man - i siz - we sin - gen - ze njani

ba - ya ja - bu - la a - basi-thanda-yo ho.___

Homeward Bound

Words and Music by PAUL SIMON

1. I'm sit-tin' in the rail-way sta-tion, got a tick-et for my
2. Ev-'ry day's an end-less stream of cig-a-rettes and
(3. To -) night I'll sing my songs a-gain, I'll play the game

dest-in-a-tion. _____ Mm _____
mag-a-zines. _____ Mm _____
and pre-tend. _____ Mm _____

On a tour___ of one night stands my suit-case and gui-tar___
And each town looks___ the same to me, the mov-ies and the fac-
But all my words___ come back to me in shades of me-di-oc-

in hand___ and ev-'ry stop is neat-ly planned___ for a
-tor-ies___ and ev-'ry strang-er's face I see___ re-
-ri-ty___ like emp-ti-ness in har-mon-ny___ I

po - et and a one___ man band._____
minds me that I long___ to be,_____
need some - one to com - fort me._____

Chorus:

Home - ward___ Bound, I wish I was,_____

How The Heart Approaches What It Yearns

Words and Music by PAUL SIMON

212

Coda

yearns.

How the heart ap-

proach - es_____ what it yearns.

rit.

I Am A Rock

Words and Music by PAUL SIMON

To the streets be - low On a fresh - ly fall - en si - lent shroud of snow.
Friend - ship caus - es pain. It's laugh - ter and it's lov - ing I dis - dain.
feel - ings that have died. If I nev - er loved I nev - er would have cried.
Safe with - in my womb. I touch no one and no one touch - es me.

I Am A Rock,__

I am an is - land.

2. I've built __
3. Don't talk of
4. I have my land. __ And a

rock feels no pain; And an is - land nev - er cries. __

I Do It For Your Love

Words and Music by PAUL SIMON

Jonah

Words and Music by PAUL SIMON

Medium Soft Rock beat

Half an hour.— Change— your strings and tune—— up.—
No one gives their dreams— a - way too light - ly.——

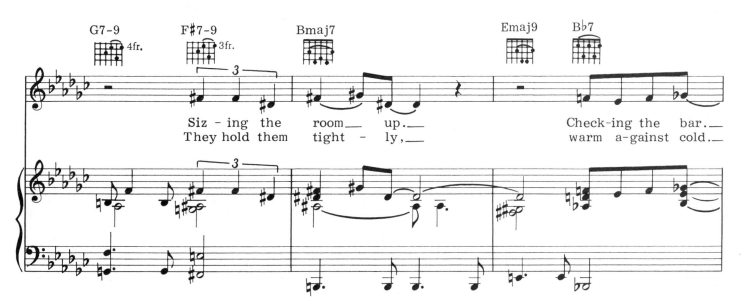

Siz - ing the room— up.— Check-ing the bar.—
They hold them tight - ly,— warm a-gainst cold.—

Do you won-der where those boys have gone?

Do you won-der where those boys have

gone?

Repeat and fade

I Know What I Know

Words by PAUL SIMON
Music by PAUL SIMON and GENERAL M.D. SHIRINDA

She

looked me o - ver and I guess she thought I was all right,

some - thing a - bout you that real - ly re - minds me of mon - ey."

moved so eas - i - ly, all I could think of was sun - light.

She was the all

I said, She was the

Kathy's Song

Words and Music by PAUL SIMON

Moderately

1. I hear the driz - zle of the rain
2. And from the shel - ter of my mind
3. My mind's dis - tract - ed and dif - fused

Like a mem - o - ry it falls
Through the win - dow of my eyes
My thoughts are man - y miles a - way

Late In The Evening

Words and Music by PAUL SIMON

Brightly, in 2

The

first thing I____ re - mem - ber, I____ was ly - ing in____ my bed.____
next thing I____ re - mem - ber, I____ am walk - in' down____ the street.____
learned to play____ some lead____ gui - tar.____ I was un - der - age____ in this

The first thing I__ re-mem-ber when you came__ __in-to my life,__ I said, "I'm gon-na get that girl__ no mat-ter what__ I do."__

Well, I

D.S. 𝄋 al Coda ⊕

Coda ⊕

Repeat and fade

Keep The Customer Satisfied

Words and Music by PAUL SIMON

It's the same old sto - ry ____
It's the same old sto - ry _____ (Yeah) }
Ev - 'ry-where I

go, _____ I get slan - dered, Li - beled, ___ I hear words ___

____ I nev - er heard in the Bi - ble. _____ And I'm one step a - head of the

shoe shine, Two steps a - way from the coun-ty line, Just trying to keep my cus - tom-ers

Kodachrome™

Words and Music by PAUL SIMON

With a moving beat

Verse 1.

1. When I think back ___ on all ___ the crap ___ I learned in high ___

___ school,   It's a won-der

cam - 'ra, I love to take a pho - to - graph, ___ So mom - ma, don't take ___

___ my Ko - da - chrome ___ a - way. ___

To next strain

No chord

Fine

2. If you took all ___

Verse 2.

___ the girls ___ I knew when I was sin - gle

Loves Me Like A Rock

Words and Music by PAUL SIMON

dent.) I say, "Now who do,___ who do you think you're fool-

(Who do you think you're fool -ing?" -ing?") I've got the Pres - i - den - tial

Seal, (Was___ the Pres - i - dent.) I'm up on the Pres - i - den - tial

Po - di - um.___ My ma - ma loves___ me, she loves___

The Late, Great Johnny Ace

Words and Music by PAUL SIMON
Coda by PHILIP GLASS

Medium shuffle

It was the year of the Bea - tles. It was the

year of the Stones. ___ It was nine - teen ___ six - ty - four.

___ I was liv -

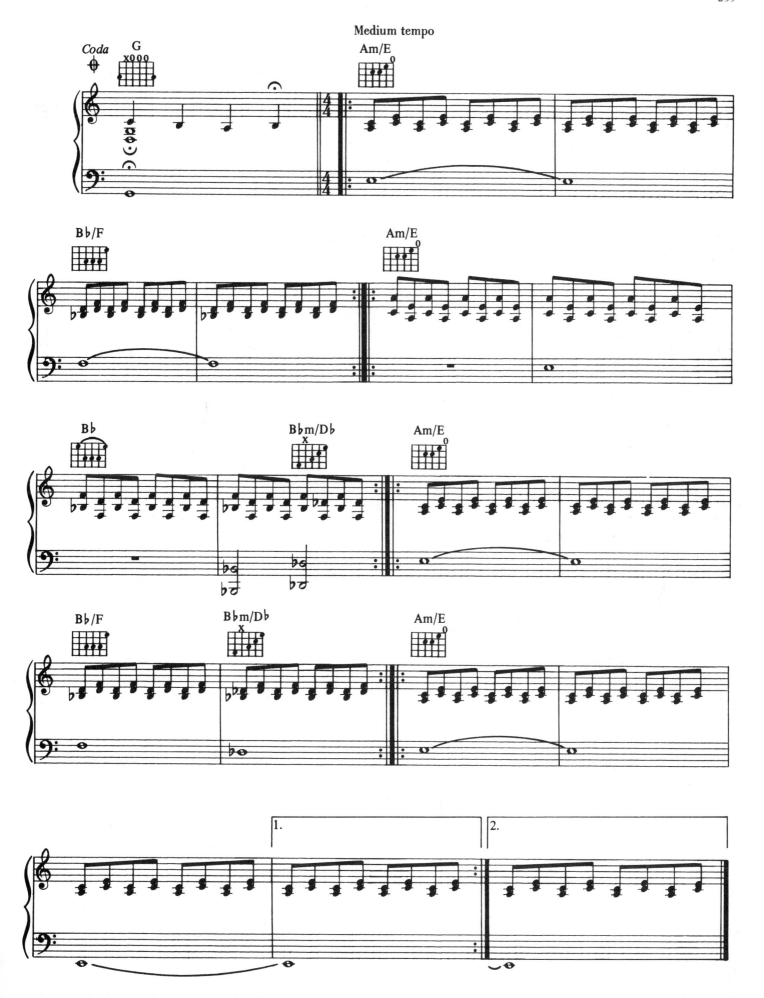

Learn How To Fall

Words and Music by PAUL SIMON

Leaves That Are Green

Words and Music by PAUL SIMON

Moderately

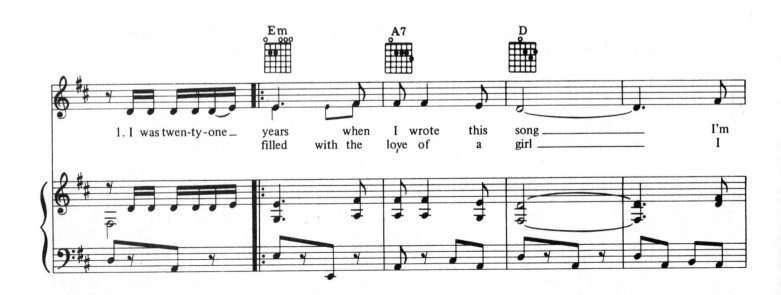

1. I was twen-ty-one — years when I wrote this song _____ I'm
filled with the love of a girl _____ I

twen-ty-two___ now   but I won't   be   for   long_____   time_____
held   her___ close,   but she fad-ed   in   the   night_____   like a   poem

___ I   hur-ries   on_____   } And the Leaves   That Are   Green_____
   meant to   write_____

___   turn   to   brown,_____   And they with-er   with the

wind,___   And   they   crum-ble   in   your   hand._____

Bm

And they with - er with the wind,__

Em7   A7   D   D.S. 𝄋 al Coda ⊕

And they crum-ble in your hand._____ 4. Hel - lo, Hel-

Coda   D   Bm

brown._____

A7   A

Long, Long Day

Words and Music by PAUL SIMON